GOD'S GREATEST GIFT

THE PROPHECIES, THE PROMISES, AND THE PEOPLE OF GOD'S REDEMPTIVE PLAN

MICHAEL STATON

Christmas: God's Greatest Gift

Layout and Cover Design by Marcy Staton

EWP Publishing

ISBN: 978-0-578-80018-9

Printed in the USA

OTHER BOOKS

BY MICHAEL STATON

Anchored In Hope:
A 40 Day Devotional

Pray Then
Like This

AVAILABLE NOW ON

EVERYWORDPREACHED.COM

FOR THESE AS WELL AS SERMON VIDEOS, DAILY DEVOTIONS, AND OTHER WRITINGS, VISIT EVERYWORDPREACHED.COM

TABLE OF CONTENTS

Dedication

Those who know my wife, Marcy, know that she honestly can do anything. She is the most talented and amazing person I have ever known. While Marcy could have done anything in her life she set her mind to do, she has chosen to make her primary avenue of service to support me and partner with me in ministry. This book is no different. She has given hours to help me in this project out of a desire to be a blessing to the body of Christ.

One of the countless things I love about my wife is that she has always made Christmas magical at our house. From opening our home to numerous guests during the holidays to making sure everything is special for our family, she continually goes the extra mile to capture the beauty and splendor of the season. She loves Jesus, cares for people, and delights in celebrating Christmas. When you put it all together, it creates the sweetest place on earth to me – our home at Christmastime.

Certainly, any good that comes from this project, or anything I do, is only because of God's grace. Humanly speaking, she is the one that makes it possible for me to do what God has called me to do. Her endless support, encouragement, and patience are such gifts to me. It is the joy of my life to serve with her in ministry, and there is no one I would rather celebrate Christmas with each year!

Michael

A Word to the Reader

The purpose of this book is to point you to Jesus as you consider the depth of God's plan to redeem the lost. Whether you read these words during the Christmas season or another time of the year, I hope it will direct your mind to the purpose of the birth of Christ and cause your faith to rest in the hope that only comes from knowing the Lord.

As you read these chapters, my prayer is that the fullness of God's redemptive plan comes alive. The story of Christmas neither starts nor ends in Bethlehem. Originating in the Garden of Eden, the story spans the centuries to Calvary and will someday culminate at the Second Coming of Jesus. The heart of Christmas is that God kept His promise to send a Redeemer who paid for our sins. There is simply no way to fully comprehend the message of Christmas without recognizing the deadly effects of sin and the glorious impact of the cross.

Have you not yet come to the place in your life where you have asked the Lord to forgive your sins? I pray the journey we take together will cause you to trust in Jesus Christ. If you are a Christian, I pray that your faith will be deepened as you perhaps, learn something new.

At the end of each chapter, you will find a story describing the circumstances behind some of our most beloved Christmas carols, along with the song lyrics. I love music, and Christmas music is my absolute favorite! I want the history of these carols to come to life and for you to better understand the story behind each song as you discover how the message of each connects with Scripture. I'm hoping the next time you sing these Christmas songs that you will do so with a greater insight into the history and circumstances that brought them to us. More importantly, I hope it adds to your knowledge of the truth of Christmas, God's greatest gift. I pray it is a blessing to you!

Introduction

Christmas is my favorite season. I enjoy everything about this holiday! Each year mid-November finds me antsy to haul the decorations down from the attic. I find myself longing for the peace that emanates from my home when it glows with lights, trees, and reminders of the joy of the season. Christmas music can be heard coming from my office beginning October first!! It's true. I even get a thrill out of crowded shopping malls, struggling to find a parking space, and battling lines as I buy gifts for friends and family.

Christmas is a time of joyful celebration. Parties, cards, and unique family traditions serve to lift the spirit and infuse the air with generosity and goodwill. For many believers (and even non-believers), Christmas reigns as the favorite day of the year.

Some years we are fully prepared to do Christmas right. Other years, things can slip through the cracks. I remember so well my first Christmas as a married man. I could not wait to celebrate Christmas with my wife, and I thought I had everything completely ready for our first Christmas day. And I did…except for the stocking. I did not know until it was too late that this was a big deal for my wife. She ended up with a stocking stuffed full of the finest treasures I could find…at midnight… from 7-11. It was the only place open.

Sometimes the same thing happens to us spiritually that happened to me that Christmas Eve night. While we have accomplished much during the Christmas season, some years we can go hurriedly along the way and not be prepared to meditate on the true meaning of the holiday. It sneaks up on us. Even Christians with the best of intentions can fail to extol the God of Christmas. In our zeal to make Christmas meaningful, we can effectually push out the very One we are meant to honor. We become distracted by twinkling lights, all the while singing about the baby born in Bethlehem, and miss the heart of the season. Who among us is not guilty of getting so enthusiastic for the shopping, wrapping, list-making, and cookie-baking that we fail to stand in awe of the glory of God's divine plan?

Let us not miss the mark this year. I invite you to deepen your knowledge of the Christmas story. As we meet the significant people and study the extraordinary events of this incredible season, I hope you will gain a more profound delight in God's great gift of Christmas. We will begin with the Old Testament prophecies of the coming Messiah as we explore the miraculous birth of Jesus. We will get to know the people who were a part of that amazing night and the events that followed. May it never be said of us that we open our hearts to the trappings of Christmas yet close our eyes to the purpose and pain of Christ's birth.

So let us decorate, sing, gather, and celebrate! God is glorified when we are joyful and loving. But as you celebrate Christmas, let the truth of God's redemptive plan cause your heart to exalt in the Lord. May our walk through the Christmas story of the Bible cause you to rest in the glorious truth that the Savior has come. May your heart truly embrace Christmas: God's greatest gift!

The Prophecies of Christmas

Christmas is a time of beloved family traditions. For many, this includes the reading of the Christmas story in Luke or Matthew. But did you know that the story in Bethlehem is only a part of God's far-reaching plan of redemption? In actuality, the story begins long before those writings. Perhaps a look at the Old Testament prophecies of Micah or Isaiah would help us understand the origins of God's plan. Actually, the prophecies of Christ pre-date even the prophets! We must begin our study of the prophecies of Christ at the beginning of all human history. As we do, we will see that Christmas is the answer to a long-awaited hope. It is the fulfillment of a promise by God to send a Savior. When the various prophecies of Christmas are examined and harmonized, the hope for the world clearly emerges: *The Redeemer will come from the tribe of Judah, a descendant of David, to be born of a virgin in the city of Bethlehem.*

The Redeemer will come...

To comprehend the fullness of Christmas, we do not begin in Bethlehem. We must go further back. The journey to Bethlehem starts in Eden. Humanity did not progress far before sinking into the mire of sin. Indeed, the first people, Adam and Eve, fell prey to the serpent's lure and disobeyed the Lord. Eve enticed Adam to sin along with her. Adam then blamed God, as well as Eve, for his sin. Together they attempted to run and hide. Both were at fault, and neither could undo their disobedience.

As a result of their sin, death has now taken center stage in the story of humanity. Apart from the gracious mercy of God, all humanity is wrecked by sin and lost for eternity. Yet God, ever faithful, stretches out His hand of hope to lift the lost from the pit of sin and bring to life those left spiritually dead. As we read Genesis 3:15, we discover the first prophet of Scripture is none other than God, Himself. Promising a redemptive Savior, He boldly confronts the author of sin: "I will put enmity between you and the woman, and between your offspring and her offspring; he shall bruise your head, and you shall bruise his heel." God, the true hero of the Bible, will provide the sacrifice for our sins. The Promised One, the serpent-crushing seed, will defeat the devil as He gives up His own body in the conflict. This is indeed the first promise of a blessed redemption, given to the first people, immediately after the introduction of sin. This *protoevangelium* (first gospel) was there from the beginning, reassuring Adam and Eve that God has a plan for the atonement of sin. The promise of Christmas is given in the Garden as man receives the gift of hope that a Redeemer will come. To trace the development of God's master plan, we need only to study the prophecies given in the Old Testament.

The Redeemer Will Come...from the Tribe of Judah

God promised Abraham that all of the world would be blessed through him (Genesis 12:1-3). This promise from God was faithfully passed down to Isaac and then to Jacob. When Jacob produced twelve sons, however, circumstances occurred that raised a question: Which son would be selected to carry on the promise?

By birthright, it should have been Reuben. But, disqualified by sin, he was passed over. The same was true for Simeon and Levi.

Then Jacob, old and near death, uttered one of the most remarkable prophecies in all of the Bible. Giving each son an appropriate blessing, he foretold the blessed significance of his fourth son's lineage. You see, although Jacob's physical eyes may have been dimmed with old age, he still saw with eyes of faith and looked toward the day when the tribe of Judah would take leadership in Israel. The people of Judah were destined to possess the courage and strength of a lion.

Scripture tells us the scepter (the sign of regal authority) will rest with Judah until "Shiloh" comes. Scholars are unsure of the precise meaning of Shiloh. The term was either a proper name for the coming Messiah, or it was a Hebrew contraction which meant, "he to whom it (the scepter) belongs."

The prophetic blessing of Jacob in Genesis 49:8-12 details four characteristics unique to the tribe of Judah, which are crucial to the Christmas story. First, Judah will be the dominant tribe in Israel (verse 8). Second, Judah will display the courage of a lion (verse 9). Third, the Messiah will come from the tribe of Judah (verse 10). Finally, the coming of the Messiah will bring peace, joy, and prosperity (verses 11-12).

The life of King David is a partial fulfillment of this prophecy, but it awaits an even greater King. The One who will come and crush the serpent's head and bring all things to subjection under His feet will be none other than David's greater Son, the Messiah Himself. And this greater Son will come not once, but twice. The first time He will come like a lamb to be slain. The second time He will come as a lion to bring judgment. The perfect restoration of peace and prosperity will take place at His second coming as He rules and reigns and defeats the powers of the devil, that serpent of old (Revelation 20:2).

One needs only to study the Old Testament to discover that these prophecies of the coming Savior set forth a recurring theme of anticipation among the Jewish people. When would the Messiah come? Like a child waiting for Christmas morning, the Israelites longed for the advent of their promised Savior. Leader after leader was appointed to authority, but none who fulfilled this ancient prophecy. Moses was of the tribe of Levi, Joshua of Ephraim, Gideon of Manasseh, Samson of Dan, Samuel of Ephraim, and Saul of Benjamin. Each was fulfilling his role of leadership, yet not destined to redeem. The Redeemer will come, and He will be of the tribe of Judah. God's promise was as certain as it was precise.

It is worth noting in the book of Revelation, the Apostle John describes Jesus as "the Lion of the tribe of Judah" (Revelation 5:5). Our Savior and King came to earth that first Christmas as a meek and mild infant. God's promise to send the Redeemer was kept. The same Redeemer will come again, not as a baby, but a triumphant King. Next time, He will not bring salvation but judgment.

The Redeemer will come from the tribe of Judah…a descendant of David

Saul, the first king of Israel, rejected God and ultimately proved his unworthiness to rule. God then replaced him with a young man named David…from the tribe of Judah. Do you know that the very first words of the New Testament mention David? Matthew 1:1

begins with, "The book of the genealogy of Jesus Christ, the son of David, the son of Abraham."

The words of 2 Samuel 7, spoken by the prophet Nathan, help us understand the fullness of what is to happen that night in Bethlehem. The prophecy recorded in 2 Samuel has both an immediate and an ultimate fulfillment. The immediate realization is that of David's son, Solomon, while the ultimate is God's Son, Jesus Christ.

The promise of verse 13, given to the prophet Nathan by the Lord, says, "I will establish the throne of his kingdom forever." We know this is not ultimately about Solomon, as his kingdom was not forever. In fact, shortly after his death, the nation of Israel is divided into two separate kingdoms. *Forever* can only be in reference to eternity. And there, Jesus Christ rules as King of Kings and Lord of Lords, without end and without rival.

Scripture records, "And your house and your kingdom shall be made *forever* before me. Your throne shall be established *forever*" (2 Samuel 7:16). The Bible clarifies that the Hope for all of the world will come through the line of David. We read again of the fulfillment of this blessed promise at Christmas in Luke 1:32-33, which states, "He will be great and will be called the Son of the Most High. And the Lord God will give to him the throne of his father David, and he will reign over the house of Jacob *forever,* and of his kingdom *there will be no end.*"

What an incredible declaration! In one sense, it all began that starry night in Bethlehem. In a truer sense, however, the Christmas story begins centuries before the appearance of shepherds and wise men. Long before Mary and Joseph would frantically search for a place to spend the night, the prophecies of Christmas were already sustaining the people of God. David is given a divine promise, fulfilled many generations later.

The Redeemer will come from the tribe of Judah, a descendant of David...and be born of a virgin

It is regrettable that in our day, it is popular to attack the teaching of the virgin birth. The notion of a chaste conception seems so outrageous, so extraordinary, so...supernatural. Be careful here, dear Christian. It is a small step from denying the virgin birth to denying the resurrection. Both are miracles beyond our power of comprehension. To deny the miraculous power of God is to deny God Himself. God created the heavens and the earth by the word of His mouth. He will see to it that every promise He made will be kept, and the Redeemer will indeed be born of a virgin.

The words of Matthew 1:21-23 (referring back to Isaiah 7:14) describe this miracle: "She will bear a Son, and you shall call his name Jesus, for he will save his people from their sins. All this took place to fulfill what the Lord had spoken by the prophet: Behold, the virgin shall conceive and bear a son, and they shall call his name Immanuel (which means, God with us). "When the story of the birth of Christ is read, it reveals the fulfillment of ancient prophecies given by God to His people. Christmas teaches us not only that God is good but also that His word can be trusted.

How did this fulfillment of the prophecy of Isaiah actually happen for Mary? Luke 1:35 describes, "The Holy Spirit will come upon you, and the power of the Most High will overshadow you; therefore the child to be born will be called holy—the Son of God." Though inexplicable to us, God's plan to knit together His holy child in a virgin's womb proves the power and genius of God. Jesus, truly God and truly man, will be born without a sin nature through the miracle of the virgin birth. He will walk where we walk and face temptations as we do, yet live without the stain of sin. His perfect life qualifies Him to be our perfect substitute on Calvary's cross. His vicarious death provides the sacrifice needed for the atonement of our sins. Amazing grace indeed!

The Redeemer will come from the tribe of Judah, a descendant of David, and be born of a virgin...in the city of Bethlehem

I have been to Bethlehem and had the privilege of walking the city where our Savior was born. Although today it seems in many ways a typical town of twenty-five thousand people, what took place two thousand years ago was far from ordinary. Though devoid of castles or breath-taking sites, Bethlehem will forever hold the honor of the birthplace of our Savior. It is both fascinating and awe-inspiring to walk the streets of a town so significant in Scripture.

While many expected the Messiah to take up residence in a palace and reign from a throne, the prophet Micah foretold that He would be born in Bethlehem, far away from any palace and nowhere near any earthly throne. Micah prophesied, "But you, O Bethlehem Ephrathath, who are too little to be among the clans of Judah, from you shall come forth for me one who is to be ruler in Israel, whose coming forth is from of old, from ancient days" (Micah 5:2).

The term *Ephrathath* is useful as it distinguishes the place of the birth of Jesus from a place in the northern part of Galilee that was also called Bethlehem. The prophecy of Micah 5:2 is that this seemingly insignificant town of Bethlehem will be the host to the most extraordinary event the world has ever seen. We read about the fulfillment of this prophecy in the well-loved passage from Luke chapter two. Here is how it all unfolded:

> In those days a decree went out from Caesar Augustus that all the world should be registered. This was the first registration when Quirinius was governor of Syria. And all went to be registered, each to his own town. And Joseph also went up from Galilee, from the town of Nazareth, to Judea, to the city of David, which is called Bethlehem, because he was of the house and lineage of David, to be registered with Mary, his betrothed, who was with child. And while they were there, the time came for her to give birth. And she gave birth to her firstborn son and wrapped him in swaddling cloths and laid him in a manger, because there was no place for them in the inn (Luke 2:1-7).

To fully understand the glory of Christmas, we must look past the lights, gifts, and traditions and go back to the prophecies that speak of this most blessed event. As church-age Christians, we have the privilege to study these prophecies ourselves and marvel at the amazing plan of redemption. Indeed, each prophecy of the Old Testament can be harmonized into one glorious statement: *The Redeemer will come from the tribe of Judah, a descendant of David, and be born of a virgin in the city of Bethlehem.* The prophecies were fulfilled, and that amazing night in Bethlehem, the good news rang out: The Savior is born. God's greatest gift has been given.

The Story of O Come O Come Emmanuel

O Come O Come Emmanuel was written some thirteen hundred years ago and was sung in formal masses in Latin. The most ancient of all Christmas carols, this beloved song is sung in church worship services by denominations all over the world today. Though history has not preserved the author's name, it is thought that he was a Catholic monk who, as a scholar, possessed a significant knowledge of the Old Testament.

Each verse of this song bridges the Old Testament promises with the truths revealed in the New Testament. During the Middle Ages, when illiteracy was rampant, *O Come O Come Emmanuel* taught the theology of the coming of the Messiah when the people could not read it for themselves.

The song's popularity is owed to an Anglican priest named John Mason Neal. A brilliant man, he spoke twenty languages. His church sent him to Africa where he founded a girl's school and an orphanage. While in Africa, he came across the old Latin verses that read, "O come Emmanuel and ransom captive Israel."

Neal translated the words of this beloved hymn from Latin into English, and the lyrics were put together with music from the fifteenth century. The piece, as it is known today, was finished in 1851 and published with five verses. When the song is sung today, the listener experiences the weight of an oppressed and desperate people who are longing for their Redeemer's appearance.

There are variations in the text of the song as it has been adapted through the years. However, each version captures the hope of a people trusting in the promises of God and waiting for the arrival of the blessed Emmanuel, God with us.

O come, O come, Emmanuel
And ransom captive Israel
That mourns in lonely exile here
Until the Son of God appear

O come, Thou Wisdom from on high
Who orderest all things mightily
To us the path of knowledge show
And teach us in her ways to go

O come, Thou Rod of Jesse, free
Thine own from Satan's tyranny
From depths of hell Thy people save

And give them victory over the grave

O come, Desire of nations, bind
In one the hearts of all mankind
Bid Thou our sad divisions cease
And be Thyself our King of Peace

Rejoice! Rejoice!
Emmanuel shall come to thee, O Israel

The Promise of Christmas

In the previous chapter, we saw that the *prophecies* concerning the Messiah offer specific details of how Jesus would come. It is also important to see how the *promises* of Isaiah 9 encourage us with the ministry He will perform and the hope He will bring. These are promises that have spanned the centuries from the birth of Christ to this very moment. It is a comfort to know God's promises as we rest in knowing that He can fulfill each one. How good it is to know that our God has the power to make light what is dark, to turn our sadness into joy, and to strengthen the weak. Isaiah is a book rich in prophecy that gives insight into the coming Messiah's character; He will be the hope for the world.

Jesus came to bring light to a world that has always loved the darkness. Despite the calamity and destruction that comes, people continually choose to stumble along blindly rather than walk by the light of God's truth. Like a parent training a child, God warns His people not to be led astray from the truth. Through the prophet Isaiah, God warns that those who look for answers apart from Him will "have no dawn" and that they will live in "distress and darkness" (Isaiah 8:20, 22).

From the moment evil entered the world in the Garden of Eden, spiritual darkness has permeated humanity. Jesus came to be the Light of the world. He was sent by the Father to break into a world of darkness and rebellion. This is the Father's promise, and it will be the Messiah's purpose.

The opening words of Isaiah 9 shockingly speak in the past tense, although they are describing events yet to take place. The word from the Lord declares, "The people who walked in darkness *have seen* a great light; those who dwelt in a land of deep darkness, on them *has light shone*." The promise of what the Messiah will bring is so certain that it can be spoken of as if it already happened.

Two lands are also mentioned: Naphtali and Zebulun. These two cities may not be familiar to many, but they are highly significant. Both cities were vulnerable to attack because of their perilous location. They were the first stop for Assyrian invaders who marched from the north to attack Israel. In the New Testament, Jesus begins His public ministry as He enters Capernaum in the area of Zebulun and Naphtali. The same land devastated by the Assyrian darkness in the Old Testament prophecy, one day beholds the Light of the world, just as had been promised.

It is a comfort for us to know that God's promises are steadfast, long-lasting, and sure. The promise of Christmas is wrapped up in the promise that the Messiah would come and bring hope to a decimated people. In Christ, God's promises are kept as the Light pierced the darkness, and God came near. As God comes near, His people experience the wonders of His love.

As light invades the darkness, there is an unleashing of joy through freedom and security. This future joy is pictured in Isaiah 9 as a farmer rejoicing in the harvest and a soldier celebrating victory in war. One day, we will no longer be endangered by the evil things of this world nor prone to wander in our sin. We will live forever with Jesus in His kingdom, where there will be no more sorrow, tears, nor death. We will have no need of the sun because Jesus will be our light.

God has a history of bringing His people out of darkness and into His light. The words of the prophet Isaiah bring to mind the well-known account of Israel's bondage in Egypt (Isaiah 9:4). It reminds us that believers have always faced adversity, yet the Lord uses His unmatched strength and power to free His people. In great joy, with singing and celebration, the children of Israel praised the Lord for His deliverance. Likewise, Isaiah describes the joy to come for those who belong to the Lord. He references the day of Midian (Isaiah 9:4), which alludes to Judges 6-8 when God demonstrated His great strength and power by reducing Gideon's army from 32,000 to only 300 men. God alone gave Israel the victory over the Midianites.

He will come in power to rescue His people once again for all eternity. The Old Testament promise is that God will always vindicate His name and provide for His own. That very same promise is alive and active in the lives of Christians today.

God demonstrates His authority and might repeatedly in Scripture so that we can know the security in which our freedom is held. In Isaiah's day, God-fearers wondered who would bring about this security that had been promised and that they so desperately longed to experience. Would it be a powerful king with a mighty army? Perhaps a wealthy man with resources more significant than the earth had witnessed?

No! The gift of God to His people that brought freedom and security was a tiny baby wrapped in swaddling clothes and lying in a manger. Incredible!

The gift of God to His people is described this way, "For to us a child is born, to us a son is given; and the government shall be upon his shoulder, and his name shall be called Wonderful Counselor, Mighty God, Everlasting Father, Prince of Peace" (Isaiah 9:6). Jesus arrived the first time as a helpless baby, cradled by human hands.

He will come again, riding on a white horse, as a conquering king. At His first coming, He was judged and sentenced to die by human authorities. One day, those very same men will bow before Jesus and acknowledge that Christ alone is the King of all Kings.

Let us look more closely at the ministry that Jesus performed. The first promise that Isaiah 9:6 gives is that the Messiah will be a "Wonderful Counselor." Jesus fulfilled this promise as He directed His people to walk in the light. He steadfastly modeled how to live in wisdom. His words and life are an example that He gave for us to follow. In the first century, Jesus was observed and emulated by His followers. Today, believers should seek the wonderful counsel of the Lord as they read of the life of Jesus and study the written Word of God.

The second promise in Isaiah 9:6 is that the Messiah will come in full force and be the embodiment of the "Mighty God" (*El Gibbor*). Christ will be the protector of those who trust in Him. The language used here describes Him as the powerful One who will defeat our enemies for us. Opposition is a part of the fallen world. Regardless of the details of our battle, our hope is the same: Jesus is the Mighty God, who is a warrior on behalf of His people. Those who believe in Jesus will rest in His power and victory.

A third promise is that the Messiah will be as an "Everlasting Father" to His people. In Isaiah's day, a king was a kind of father to the nation. The coming Savior will adopt believers into His family and protect and provide for His people. The description of Everlasting Father details the manner of care that He will provide. The coming Savior will possess unwavering compassion and tenderness for His children. Our Savior will protect, sustain, defend, and comfort us. As a strong and compassionate father serves and leads his family, so our Savior will care for us.

Finally, Isaiah 9:6 promises that God's Anointed One will be the "Prince of Peace." Christ's compassionate love for believers plants a seed of peace in our hearts that strengthens all who receive it. As peace bears its fruit, God's character is magnified. Jesus is indeed the Prince of Peace.

The peace of God serves a dualistic purpose in the life of a believer. Those who belong to Him experience a feeling of inner peace, knowing that we are His, and nothing can ever take us out of His caring hand. However, not only does He give us peace in our spirits, but He brings us peace in our standing with God the Father. Through His sacrificial death on the cross, Jesus did what no mortal man could do. He made a way for sinners to be at peace with God, no longer under wrath as an enemy.

Do not be fooled by counterfeit offers of peace. In Jeremiah 6, God indicted the prophets and priests of the day as He exclaimed, "They have healed the wound of my people lightly, saying, 'Peace, peace' when there is no peace." Only God authors true peace, and He did just that by sending His Son, Jesus. Genuine peace within your own heart can only come from having a right relationship with God. And that relationship with the Father can only come through the work of the Son.

Made available through Jesus, the promise of peace was on the lips of the angels the night Christ was born. Scripture records the angelic announcement to the shepherds on the night of Christ's birth when they proclaimed, "Glory to God in the highest, and on earth peace among those with whom he is pleased." Jesus indeed is the Prince of Peace.

Think of how hopeful and needed this promise of Isaiah 9:6 would be for God's people through the centuries that would follow. Remember, a few years after this prophecy recorded in Isaiah, in 722 BC, the Assyrians will come and sack the northern kingdom of Israel. The people of God will need the hope of God's prophecies and promises to get them through this bleak chapter of their history.

At times they will be tempted to think they have been forsaken and that they are left without a Savior. But God keeps His promises. Though the birth of Christ will tarry for seven more centuries after Isaiah pens the words, the One who will be the Wonderful Counselor, Mighty God, Everlasting Father, and Prince of Peace most assuredly will come. God's people will not be abandoned nor left without hope.

On the day of Israel's destruction by Assyria, the light of hope was all but extinguished. Then, a century after the northern kingdom was abolished, the Babylonians demolished the southern kingdom of Judah. Never have things looked darker. Yet amid this present darkness and coming disasters, the promise of hope is still found in the words of Isaiah. No matter how difficult life becomes, and regardless of the world's condition, the promised Messiah will come, and He will accomplish all He was sent to do. His kingdom will come, and it will last. Isaiah prophesied about the coming Messiah, saying, "Of the increase of his government and of peace there will be no end, on the throne of David and over his kingdom, to establish it and to uphold it with justice and righteousness from this time forth and forevermore. The zeal of the Lord of hosts will do this." (Isaiah 9:7). In a world wrecked by sin and full of turmoil, the true people of God in Isaiah's day clung to the promises of Scripture. Today, we must do the same!

The Story of In the Bleak Midwinter

Beautifully haunting, the lyrics to *In the Bleak Midwinter* are as penetrating as they are poetic. The song captures the hope of humanity now that the Savior has come to a desperate and dying world.

The words of this Christmas hymn were authored by Christina Rosetti. Born in 1830, she lived in England as a poet and devotional writer. Having never married, much of her life was spent in serving others while she herself suffered from Grave's disease. She would later battle cancer, which would eventually lead to her death at the age of 64.

Before it was a Christmas song sung worldwide, *In the Bleak Midwinter* was a poem initially entitled, *A Christmas Carol*, and first published in 1872 in a holiday issue of *Scribner's Monthly*. It would be thirty-four years later, and twelve years after her death, that the poem would be set to music by composer Gustav Holst.

The song describes a dispirited earth in need of a Savior. Using the backdrop of an unrelenting winter, Rosetti describes the condition of humanity as a frigid day in the dead of winter. Water has frozen solid as temperatures plummet. The winds howl as the unrelenting snow falls more and more. This is not the picturesque scene of a Rockwell painting. No! This is the snow that continually blankets the earth leaving its inhabitants without the ability to escape. It is an apt picture of humanity and our sin. Without a Savior, we too are unable to survive, thoroughly covered over, blanketed in despair, wearied, and without hope.

The hope of Christmas, though, is that darkness gives way to light, and death gives way to life. God the Father sent His only Son, Jesus, the Messiah, into the winter of our souls that we might find hope, joy, love, and peace.

The song's final verse takes us back to the night the Christ-child was born. Do you remember the invited guests that met Jesus that first Christmas night? The lowly shepherds. Suppose you were a poor shepherd. What gift could you bring to the King of Kings? Perhaps you could offer a lamb as an offering of worship. You are familiar with the wise men who traveled from the east. What if you were a wise man? What could you do as an act of worship? Well, you could do your part to help the family.

But the question for you this Christmas season is not what would a shepherd offer,nor what should a wise man bring. The question is simply, *what will you give to Jesus*? The closing words of the song's final verse implore you to lay before Him the only thing He asks of you: *your heart.*

In the bleak mid-winter
Frosty wind made moan
Earth stood hard as iron
Water like a stone
Snow had fallen, snow on snow
Snow on snow
In the bleak mid-winter
Long ago

Our God, Heaven cannot hold Him
Nor earth sustain
Heaven and earth shall flee away
When He comes to reign
In the bleak mid-winter
A stable-place sufficed
The Lord God Almighty
Jesus Christ

What can I give Him
Poor as I am
If I were a Shepherd
I would bring a lamb
If I were a Wise Man
I would do my part
Yet what I can I give Him
Give my heart

The Pronouncements of Christmas

Among the most remarkable aspects of the Christmas story are the angelic announcements that took place. Many times in Scripture, the Lord dispatched one of His angels to proclaim the work that God was doing and instruct the hearer. These encounters are as amazing as they are enlightening. The Christmas story is rich in these heavenly messages, most especially in the lives of Mary, Joseph, and the shepherds. These angelic encounters have inspired many songwriters, artists, and authors. In fact, some of the most beloved Christmas songs speak to these heavenly messengers as they capture the imaginations of people all around the world.

God sent the angel, Gabriel, to appear to a young Israelite girl named Mary. It seems that Gabriel is a favorite messenger angel of God. Six months earlier, he had also appeared to Zechariah, a high priest who had a barren wife, Elizabeth. Luke details Mary's encounter with Gabriel, which would change her life forever. Gabriel's task was to tell her she was highly favored by God and would carry the Christ-child.

The Angelic Pronouncement to Mary

In the sixth month the angel Gabriel was sent from God to a city of Galilee named Nazareth (Luke 1:26)

The reference to the "sixth month" is letting the biblical reader know that Elizabeth, the barren wife of Zechariah, and Mary's cousin, is now in her sixth month of pregnancy with a son who will become known as John the Baptist. For readers of that day, it is quite puzzling that the angel would now come to Nazareth, a small village of only a few hundred people. This town was not known for much, except perhaps immorality. A remote area, Nazareth had been taken over by the Romans and turned into a haven for soldiers. It is of this place that Nathaniel, a follower of Christ, scoffed, "Can anything good come out of Nazareth?" (John 1:46).

The fact that the story of the birth of the Messiah would involve Nazareth is a clear reminder that Jesus is not coming merely to save the elite, the prosperous, or the educated. Even those who confessed Him as the Son of God were taken aback at His hometown! Jesus was unconcerned with these things, however. He did not come to impress the crowds. Rather, He came to save sinners. This is the good news of Christmas. The Messiah has come, and He has reached down to identify with the most humble and lowly. Praise be to God!

...to a virgin betrothed to a man whose name was Joseph of the house of David (Luke 1:27)

In that day, there were essentially three stages of a Jewish marriage. First was the choice of a mate, then betrothal, and last was the wedding ceremony. During the betrothal period, which lasted about a year, a Jewish couple was considered to be lawfully united. They could only dissolve their betrothal by a certificate of divorce. The man and woman were not, however, to consummate their union during this time.

Scripture makes clear that Joseph was of the house of David. The genealogy recorded in Matthew establishes the claim of Jesus to the throne of David because Jesus would be Joseph's legal heir. God is clearly bringing all of the details together that would fulfill each Old Testament prophecy concerning the Messiah. These fulfillments would later serve as one of the validating factors of the earthly ministry of Jesus.

...and the virgin's name was Mary (Luke 1:27)

It is simply astounding that this life-changing event will take place through a young, poor girl. In a culture where rich men ruled, all three of those attributes were looked down upon, but God delights in revealing His glory in unlikely situations. Mary is God's exact choice to be the earthly mother of Jesus.

Confused, Mary is stunned at the angel's message. Luke says she was "greatly troubled" (Luke 1:29). How could she *not* be? The culture of her day certainly did not value her type. Never had she heard of a young, poor girl who was bestowed with an honor. Further, Mary had never seen an angel before, and how could she ever believe the message that had been given to her?

The angel comforted the young girl by assuring her that she had found favor in the eyes of God. The announcement was unmistakable: "you will conceive in your womb and bear a son, and you shall call his name Jesus. He will be great and will be called the Son of the Most High. And the Lord God will give to him the throne of his father David, and he will reign over the house of Jacob forever, and of his kingdom there will be no end" (Luke 1:31-33). This ordinary girl was chosen to carry inside her womb the Son of God whose hands had made all that ever existed. Amazing!

How will this be, since I am a virgin? (Luke 1:34)

Certainly, Mary's heart longs to accept this honor without argument, yet logic and curiosity urge her to seek out more information. Mary has been faithful to Joseph and has remained a virgin. How could she become pregnant while faithful in her commitment to purity before God and Joseph? Gabriel gently explains that "the Holy Spirit will come upon you and the power of the Most High will overshadow you" (Luke 1:35). This response does not answer every question in Mary's mind, nor ours, but it did serve to reassure her that God had a plan, and something truly divine was taking place.

Although she knew she was participating in God's plan, Mary's mind must have been in turmoil. It is easy to imagine many of the questions she must have thought. *What will I tell my parents? Will they believe me? How do I break this news to Joseph? Will he honor our betrothal after he hears this?*

All of this news must seem unthinkable to Mary. An angelic announcement. A virgin birth. A teenager from a nowhere town chosen to be the mother of the Messiah. It all seems so unlikely and nearly impossible to comprehend. The angel comforts Mary with a final promise: "For nothing will be impossible with God" (Luke 1:37).

The Angelic Pronouncement to Joseph

Of course, the story of Christmas involved Joseph as well. His life had also been turned upside down. He had been betrothed to Mary, and all seemed to be going well, until…he found out Mary was pregnant! The biblical text clarifies that Joseph is not the father, as he kept Mary pure throughout their betrothal period. He was left to assume, as did everyone else in town, that Mary had been unfaithful to him. His disappointment and shame must have been overwhelming.

Though he had the legal right to do otherwise, he desired to deal with her *assumed* sin with compassion. This is simply who Joseph was. Joseph is described as a "just man and unwilling to put her to shame" who "resolved to divorce her quietly" (Matthew 1:19). Remember that a Jewish betrothal in that day was binding. A couple had to divorce to break the commitment. He could have chosen to do this in a public way that would have brought Mary much shame and embarrassment. That was not Joseph's heart, however.

As Joseph wrestled with how to proceed in a deliberate yet gracious manner, an angelic messenger from God appeared to him. As if a pregnant fiancé was not complicated enough, he will be told by the angel that everything is happening according to God's plan. How can this be? He would need the power of God both to comprehend and accept this strange turn his life has taken.

An angel of the Lord appeared to him in a dream, saying, 'Joseph, son of David, do not fear to take Mary as your wife, for that which is conceived in her is from the Holy Spirit.' (Matthew 1:20)

This was a bittersweet announcement for Joseph. In one regard, it surely brought him comfort to know for certain that Mary had been faithful to him. He was undoubtedly relieved that a divorce was not required. Yet the angel's words have also stirred the waters of self-doubt. How will he raise the Son of God? Who could be equal to such a task? Of all the planning Joseph had done to begin his new life with Mary, preparing to raise God's Son as his own was an unforeseen and overwhelming responsibility.

As Joseph contended with inner doubts, he knew he must also deal with the reaction of the community. Although the angel had made it clear that Mary was pure (remember that Gabriel has described Mary as having found favor with God), Joseph could only assume that they may never convince other people it was true. The angel did not appear to any of the townspeople. Who would believe such a story? Friends and family would undoubtedly hear their news and conclude that either Mary and Joseph were sinful together, or that Mary was unfaithful to Joseph. Perhaps anticipating the accusations and condemnations, Mary hurried to the town of her cousin for an extended visit. Surrounded by doubts and accusations, it will only be heaven's approval that would sustain Mary and Joseph during this difficult call to obedience.

She will bear a son, and you shall call hid name Jesus, for he will save his people from their sins (Matthew 1:21)

Although the angelic pronouncement will certainly cause difficulties for the couple, it is also joyous! The gospel story was unfolding right before their eyes. For centuries, God's people had waited for the long-expected Redeemer to come. The blood of countless animals had been poured out as they looked toward that one day that God would send the final, perfect sacrifice to atone for sin. Now the waiting is over, the Lamb is on His way. Mary and Joseph will have the honor of raising the Savior in their home.

The name *Jesus* is the Greek equivalent of Yeshua, a Hebrew name meaning, "Jehovah saves." The salvation for humanity will be wrapped up in this tiny baby. Mary and Joseph will be tasked with raising the Savior of the world. Every time they speak their son's name, they will be reminded that, though their little boy, Jesus is the sin-bearer who alone can save.

The promise of forgiveness and the hope of salvation are wrapped up in the name, Jesus. Suppose you received a check today for one million dollars. Depending on who wrote it, you would either be elated or chuckle at the joke. Most could never pay that debt and could not come through on a million-dollar promise. But if the name at the bottom of that check belonged to the CEO of Amazon or the founder of Facebook, your life would change forever. Those men have the resources to deliver the promise contained on a check of such an amount. What makes the difference? It is the name. Better said, it is the guaranteed resources associated with the name.

So it is with the promise of salvation. As Acts 4:12 boldly declares, "And there is salvation in no one else, for there is no other *name* under heaven given among men by which we must be saved." Others may promise to bring salvation, but only in Jesus will it be truly found. This baby that will be carried and delivered by Mary will not be just another prophet. He will be the very Savior of the world. Her baby will be her Redeemer. She will soon deliver Him. He will one day deliver her.

All this took place to fulfill what the Lord had spoken by the prophet: 'Behold, the virgin shall conceive and bear a son, and they shall call his name Immanuel' (which means, God with us). Matthew 1:23

All that was unfolding between Mary and Joseph was precisely what the Lord had determined to do. The story is thrilling, the plot is world-changing, and God is in complete control. God's plan is strange and unprecedented. Yet Jesus will be the very embodiment of God, and He will be with mankind. God in the flesh and God with us. Salvation has come! In this promise, Joseph found comfort. In this truth, believers today still find their rest.

The Angelic Pronouncement to the Shepherds

Everything about the Christmas story is wholly unexpected. A virgin will be overshadowed by the Holy Spirit and conceive. The explanation of what is to take place will be delivered to a young teenage girl of no social standing. The man she is betrothed to will be convinced not to divorce her by another angelic announcement. This is certainly not the way anyone expected the story of salvation to unfold.

The birth of Jesus triggers another event equally hard to believe. The first invitation to come and see that the Savior had arrived was given to shepherds. The angel of God appeared to shepherds while they were keeping watch over their flocks at night. Shepherds? Men who did such menial work were not even respected enough to testify in court in that day. Their work made them ceremonially unclean and socially rejected. Shepherds were never invited to anything until that blessed night in Bethlehem.

Yet isn't this exactly how God works? While the world fawns and feigns over the wealthy and powerful, God reaches down to the lowest and invites them to His table. No one is so prosperous that they do not need God, and no one is so lowly that they cannot be forgiven. Though overlooked by the world, the shepherds will be eyewitnesses to the most incredible event known to man.

And the angel said to them, 'Fear not, for behold, I bring you good news of great joy that will be for all the people.' (Luke 2:10)

The first instruction that the angel gave the shepherds was *fear not.* It is interesting that this command is the most frequent direction given in Scripture. The words are fitting as the shepherds, in fact, had been overcome with trepidation and fled with fear. But all that transpired that night was a manifestation of God's love for humanity. As 1 John 4:18 tells us, perfect love casts out fear.

Rather than words of judgment, as they may have been accustomed to, the shepherds heard the most glorious news ever spoken. The heavenly messenger triumphantly proclaimed, "for unto you is born this day in the city of David a Savior, who is Christ the Lord" (Luke 2:11). This simple message contains rich theology and hope for those who believe. The baby that they rushed to see was born with a mission to bring salvation. *He is the Savior.* This child bears a title: Anointed One. *He is the Christ.* He is born with a holy nature. *He is the Lord.* Jesus is the Savior, the Christ, and the Lord. And the lowly men who society had forgotten are invited to come and meet Him!

The shepherds, who had likely never been invited to anything, received the most important invitation in the history of the world that night. They were to come and greet the Savior of the world. They were not given directions to a palace or a rich man's home. No! They were instructed to find a baby wrapped in swaddling clothes and lying in a manger. Palaces and luxury were unfamiliar to them, but stables and mangers were a world they knew. And they eagerly set out to meet the Savior who had been born.

Glory to God in the highest, and on earth peace among those with whom he is pleased! (Luke 2:14)

A multitude of the heavenly hosts appeared and poured out their praise to God. All that unfolded that night in Bethlehem was a demonstration of the power and grace of the Lord. God had kept His promise. Humanity was not doomed in their sin. A way had been made, and God was glorified on earth as He is in Heaven.

Within the message of the angels is a clear picture of hope for believers today. You, too, have received an invitation to come and behold Jesus. While the world may be quick to overlook you, God has not. The invitation of Christmas still echoes throughout the world: Come and see!

How will you respond this Christmas? Let the story of Mary, Joseph, and the shepherds compel you to do as they did. May you hear the Word of God recorded in Scripture and respond with a heart of worship.

The Story of Hark! The Herald Angels Sing

Originally titled *Hymn of Christmas Day*, Charles Wesley wrote the lyrics to *Hark! The Herald Angels Sing* in 1738 at the age of thirty-two. Had it not been for a printer trying to fill some additional space, this beloved carol may have never become the well-known hymn we love. The Church of England's *Book of Common Prayer* needed more content, so the words to Wesley's song were included.

Interestingly, the opening line of the song, as we know it, is not in its original form. The first verse was changed by the famed evangelist George Whitefield. He replaced the original opening line of "Hark how all the welkin rings" to, "Hark! The herald angels sing." Ironically, Charles Wesley did not like the changes made by Mr. Whitefield and did not enjoy singing his own song.

The hymn was sung to various tunes for many years, never catching on in any significant way. That all changed in 1855 when a teenage opera singer named William Cummings found the perfect melody. While singing an opera by Felix Mendelssohn that was a tribute to the inventor of the printing press, he realized the opera's second chorus had a tune that would be the perfect fit for the Christmas hymn written by Charles Wesley over one hundred years earlier. Once these special lyrics were combined with the music, it did not take long for the song to become a regular part of congregational singing worldwide.

The development of this hymn is fascinating to consider. It was originally written by one of the most exceptional hymn writers the church has known, adapted by one of the greatest evangelists the world has seen, and set to music from an opera in celebration of one of the most significant inventions ever achieved. Although it took over a century to harmonize into the song we sing each Christmas, we now have one of the finest declarations of the proclamation of the gospel and Christmas story ever to be written.

Hark! the herald angels sing
"Glory to the newborn King
Peace on earth and mercy mild
God and sinners reconciled"
Joyful, all ye nations rise
Join the triumph of the skies
With angelic host proclaim
"Christ is born in Bethlehem"

Hark! the herald angels sing
"Glory to the newborn King"

Christ, by highest heaven adored
Christ the everlasting Lord
Late in time behold Him come
Offspring of a virgin's womb
Veiled in flesh, the Godhead see
Hail the incarnate Deity
Pleased as man with men to dwell
Jesus, our Emmanuel
Hark! the herald angels sing
"Glory to the newborn King"

Hail! the heaven-born Prince of Peace
Hail! the Son of Righteousness
Light and life to all He brings
Risen with healing in His wings
Mild He lays His glory by
Born that man no more may die
Born to raise the sons of earth
Born to give them second birth
Hark! the herald angels sing
"Glory to the newborn King"

The People of Christmas

Once the angelic pronouncements were given to Mary, Joseph, and the shepherds, it fell to them to respond. God communes with His people for many purposes, whether to inform, encourage, or even rebuke. The responsibility of the believer is always the same: to acknowledge God's instructions and take action. Let us consider in greater detail the response that each had to the heavenly news. As you remember how God's people responded in obedience on the first Christmas, let it inspire you to respond to the Lord in obedience during your own Christmas season.

To be sure, the focus of the Christmas story is Jesus, and He is the only character in the story worthy of worship. Yet there is much to be learned from the others who played a role in the unfolding drama of Christ's birth. Mary, for example, serves as a faithful lesson of trust in the Lord, even when God's plan doesn't seem to make sense.

We must remember that Mary was thrust into a very difficult position. In an instant, her trust in the Lord was tested, her emotions unsettled, and her social standing, precarious. Indeed, she was given an incredible privilege, but not one without significant struggles. If she was presumed to have been unfaithful to Joseph, he had the right to divorce her at the very least and to condemn her publicly if he so desired. Mary's own family could have rejected her and essentially left her with a lifetime of begging for survival. Yet our God, in His sovereignty, chose the right people with hearts that trusted Him to fulfill His great plan. He would not be thwarted by unwilling spirits or social customs of the day. Our God is never concerned for the outcome!

Despite facing the doubts of those who would hear her story, Mary chose to be submissive to the Lord's plan. She did not consult with anyone nor ask for time to consider her response. Her obedient spirit is conveyed in the answer she gives to Gabriel as she says with trembling faith, "Behold I am the servant of the Lord; let it be to me according to your word" (Luke 1:38). While the heart of the Christmas story celebrates the fact that God sent His only Son to earth, it is also a picture of obedient and submissive worshipers acknowledging and following the leadership of their Maker. There is much to be learned from their example.

Mary believed the word of the Lord and trusted in His plan. Think of all she did *not* yet know. She had no idea how Joseph would respond. She could not conceive what the response of her parents would be. Would her closest friends lose faith in her? Would those in her community slander her behind her back? All of these worries plus, so many more could have taken root in her mind, eventually growing and choking out the faith she held in God's plan.

But despite all the uncertainty, she believed. If the Lord were in this, surely He would make a way. Mary did not need to have all the answers in order to believe in the Lord. She only needed to know she belonged to Him. Mary's submissive spirit is evidence of her belief in her God. She vows that she is the servant of the Lord. This is no easy vow. Her submission to her Master will cost her much. But her confidence in God far outweighed her concerns for herself. She chose to trust in His word and rest in His plan. She told Him so in a beautiful prayer of worship.

The prayer of praise in Luke 1 is one of the most moving in all of Scripture. It is known as the *Magnificat* (named after the Latin translation of the first Greek word that appears in the prayer). "My soul magnifies the Lord," is the response of a sincere young girl. Her mind, chaotic with many questions, is comforted as her heart is calmed with one answer: God is trustworthy!

Much of Mary's prayer comes from the Old Testament Scripture that she obviously knew well. As she lifts her heart to extol the Lord, she draws from 1 Samuel 1:1-2, Psalm 24:8, 34, 103:17, 107, 138, and Isaiah 41. In fact, there are a dozen different Old Testament passages used in her song. The words of Scripture that she had been taught had penetrated her mind and settled deep within her heart. She finds comfort in God's Word and then turns the Scripture she knows into an expression of worship. Mary exhibited confidence in her Lord and knowledge of His Word as she positioned herself to be used for God's glory. Rightly did the angel Gabriel greet her as "favored one." Oh, that we, too, would memorize God's Word and meditate deeply on the truths it contains as we pour out our worship to Him.

Mary is not the only individual worthy of our consideration. We must also look to Joseph. It seems Joseph is often perceived as a one-dimensional character in the Christmas story. There is little information about him in the New Testament. He was present at the birth of Christ and is referenced again in Luke 2:41-52 when Jesus was found listening to teachers in the temple as a young boy. After this event, however, Joseph fades away. By the time Jesus was arrested and crucified, there is no mention of him. Surely, he had passed away by the time the events of the cross took place.

Although the earthly father of Jesus played a less dramatic role, he wasn't just there to guide the donkey to Bethlehem. We would be remiss to ignore the worthy qualities of this exceptional man. Most people associate Joseph as nothing more than a bearded man who appears in the nativity scene in a disconnected sort of way. While much is made of Mary, Joseph remains little known and mostly forgotten. Yet he steadfastly stood with Mary as a model to believers of a compassionate and obedient man.

In Matthew 1, we read that Joseph was just and righteous. He cared deeply about doing things the right and honorable way. In fact, it is this very strength of character that creates so much angst in his heart. He is torn between the social expectations he faces and the compassion he feels deeply for his betrothed. Because he was righteous, he knew he could not go through with his planned marriage to Mary if she had been unfaithful to him. Although he had every legal right to rid himself of her, he had no desire to shame or humiliate her. In kindness to her, he chose to treat her with compassion.

Joseph had every reason to believe Mary had been unfaithful to him. While her life and character had given him no reason to suspect she would do such a thing, the evidence of a pregnant fiancé would soon be obvious to all. Knowing he had not consummated their union; he was left to conclude that she had been untrue. What a devastating situation for such a good man!

Joseph had the law and logic on his side. While Mary had a wild tale of dreams, angels, and spirits, he certainly could not be blamed for harboring skepticism towards her, if not an outright concern for her mental state. As the evidence of Mary's condition became increasingly obvious, Joseph had a decision to make. Even before the angel appeared to Joseph, he had already resolved to treat her with kindness. He did not give in to the fleshly desire for revenge but instead made the decision to divorce her quietly. It would seem that Joseph cared for Mary despite her alleged offense, and so, having no desire to add unnecessary shame to her, he continued on with what he felt was the right thing to do. Yet he did so with compassion.

Of course, as the modern-day reader, we know the story from beginning to end. We know that Mary was innocent, but at that moment, Joseph did not. All he knew for sure was that Mary had told him she was pregnant, and he knew he was not the father. There did not seem to be many options to consider. His gracious character shines as he desires to ease the difficult journey on which Mary finds herself. He, the offended party -- or so he assumed -- chose gentleness over retribution and mercy over vengeance. It is little wonder he was chosen to be the earthly father of the Messiah.

Joseph's actions demonstrate one of the best aspects of the Christmas season for us today. Something about the holidays inspires people to put the well-being of others above themselves. It doesn't seem to last throughout the year, but for a short period of time, it is lovely to see. People tend to be more gracious and compassionate at Christmas. It seems that forgiveness and kindness come more easily during the season, allowing relationships to be reconciled. Undoubtedly everyone knows *someone* who needs compassion. Oh, that we would treat others with grace, thereby emulating Joseph's example! What could be better at Christmastime than to pour out your compassion on those who may not deserve it? And like Joseph, it may just be that you do not fully understand all someone else is going through at the moment. Choose to be gracious!

Perhaps because of Joseph's just behavior towards Mary, God mercifully put his doubts to rest by sending His angel to reassure Joseph of His plan. Certainty can be a precious gift to a mind that is riddled with doubt. Having received an angelic message of his own, Joseph was obedient to God in every way possible. First, "he did as the angel of the Lord commanded him" (Matthew 1:24). As Mary did, Joseph believed the word from God and responded in clear and immediate obedience. He did not push her away but solidified his allegiance to Mary, and even more so, to God's plan.

Understand that, like Mary, his obedience would come at a high price. He undoubtedly heard the sneers and taunts from people who would never believe their story. Joseph dealt with the skeptics who questioned Mary's character. He most likely endured unsolicited advice from people regarding what he should have done and how he should have handled the situation. Yes, obedience was costly, but the assurance of God's plan held greater value.

Joseph faced an even greater test of his obedience as Scripture records, "he took his wife, but knew her not until she had given birth to a son" (Matthew 1:25). Joseph's behavior towards Mary was holy and pure from the time of the angelic announcement until it was proper to consummate their marriage. It would have been tempting, and without any earthly consequence, to disobey. Joseph again chose to live in submission to God's plan. Joseph faced public condemnation as well as private temptation. Yet obedience prevailed as his confidence in God's plan strengthened him until the birth of Jesus. Would you choose to live like Joseph this Christmas season and obey the Lord no matter the consequences?

Believers must have a godly response to temptation even when no one is looking. Even when there is seemingly no earthly consequence for our sin, we must remain faithful. We would do well to follow Joseph's example and live in obedience to the will of the Lord, even if God is the only One who sees. His approval alone is sufficient motivation as we follow His direction.

A third example of obedience comes to us from the shepherds. Many people are drawn to them as they read the Christmas story.

The wise men, who arrived much later, with their entourage and expensive gifts, have little in common with most people. But the shepherds, who have little of this world, seem to resonate with us each December as they trek through the second chapter of Luke. While they may have been overlooked by society, these simple sheep watchers ignite the Christmas story with their joyful obedience and passionate worship. We can relate to them!

It was a night of angelic celebration! A group of common shepherds had a front-row seat to the announcement of the great news of the birth of Christ. Not only did they hear of this extraordinary event, they actually received an invitation to come and see the baby who was born. Perhaps they could have come up with numerous excuses for why they should wait. *The time commitment was too great. They were busily occupied with work. They could go when it was a bit more convenient.* They could have offered the same excuses so many people give today to explain their indifference to God. But these men did not.

They wholeheartedly accepted the invitation of the angel and left immediately. Luke 2:16 describes their enthusiasm this way: "And they went *with haste* and found Mary and Joseph, and the baby lying in a manger." Haste! In English, the word haste is defined as "excessive speed or urgency of movement or action; hurry." The shepherds were in a great hurry to obey God. Are you?

Many Christians who give little time and attention to the Bible's teaching do not consider themselves to be disobedient; they always see themselves as *about* to respond…just not yet. However, delayed obedience is disobedience. The time to obey the call of God is always right now. Is there something you know the Lord has called you to do that you keep putting off? Maybe the message of Christmas for you this year is to obey the Lord…with haste. No more delays!

The Book of Matthew will later record a model prayer that Jesus prayed, "Let your will be done on earth as it is in heaven" (Matthew 6:10). How is God's will performed in heaven? Immediately! We live in obedience when we mimic the response of the shepherds and obey everything the Lord has revealed to us in His Word. Let it be said this Christmas that God's people obeyed Him quickly, publicly, and fully.

The shepherds began the short journey to find the baby, and they did not stop until they arrived. Finding Mary, Joseph, and baby Jesus, the shepherds told them about the message of the angels. Can you imagine the conversation?

Each person around the manger that night had a personal story of God's amazing plan to tell. As each told of their heavenly encounters, their hearts were bonded together through their shared encounters with God. All of the people gathered around the Savior of the world surely took turns sharing how they had been blessed to be a part of the greatest event the world had seen. Undoubtedly, the faith of Mary, Joseph, and the shepherds were all strengthened as they shared personal accounts of how the Lord was at work. God was in this, and now God was with them in the flesh. Of all the blessings God has ever bestowed on His people, Jesus is the greatest gift ever given.

The shepherds teach us the value of not only quick obedience but also full obedience. It seems many people today excel at partial obedience. The call to love our family? We can handle that one. But the charge to love our enemies? Perhaps not. We may be quick to obey the command to use our spiritual gifts to serve others. But what about the call to forgive those who have hurt us or to bless those who insult us? Too often, we are not in a hurry to obey the complete counsel of God’s Word. It may be that we offer partial obedience more times than we wish when God demands our obedience in full.

Perhaps an overlooked detail of the Christmas story is the behavior of the shepherds *after* leaving the manger scene. Luke 2:20 says, "And the shepherds returned, glorifying and praising God for all they had heard and seen." Their obedience led to a special blessing, which, in turn, led to passionate worship. How often we murmur and complain about the interruptions and inconveniences of life rather than choose to praise the Lord for the privilege of being a part of His work.

The shepherds were no doubt changed that night, and their focus remained wholly on God. It is discouraging to consider how people in our self-obsessed world might respond in the same situation. Remember, the hero of the story is the Lord, and the shepherds are content to direct all attention heavenward. Some will believe their story and rejoice, while others will reject it and mock. Either way, the shepherds were quick to speak faithfully of all they had heard and seen. We would do well to follow in their footsteps.

In the example of the shepherds, we find simplicity in personal evangelism. We are invited to come and see. Then we are commissioned to go and tell. We must resist the temptation to make it more complicated than that. Come and see Christ. Learn of His grace and mercy. Receive Him as Savior and Lord. Then, go and tell. Speak of what the Lord has done for you, and tell how others can have their sin forgiven by the Savior of the world. May our lives be like that of the shepherds.

This Christmas season, choose to be like Mary, who was submissive, believing, and worshipful. Decide that this year you will live like Joseph in righteousness, compassion, and obedience. Finally, commit to emulating the shepherds by being quick to respond, obeying the Lord fully, and glorifying God in all things!

The Story of O Little Town of Bethlehem

One of the most peaceful Christmas carols of all time was ironically birthed during the tragic chaos of war. *O Little Town of Bethlehem* was written by Phillips Brooks, a highly respected leader and evangelist who loved people with deep affection. He served as the rector of the Church of the Holy Trinity in Philadelphia, Pennsylvania. Brooks never married but poured himself into church ministry.

Brooks was known for such thought-provoking words as, "Do not pray for tasks equal to your powers. Pray for powers equal to your task." He also once said, "I do not pray for a lighter load, but for a stronger back." He is best known among preachers for his definition of what preaching should be: *truth through personality*.

During his ministry, the American Civil War broke out, affecting not only his congregation, but taking a toll on Brooks personally. As families relied upon Brooks for counseling and care, his spirit began to collapse. Though physically imposing, his heart could not endure the sorrow of that time. He became understandably overwhelmed.

Facing complete exhaustion, both physically and spiritually, he sought to rejuvenate his spirit while on sabbatical. It was during this season of his life that the thirty-year-old minister found his way to the Holy Land. On Christmas Eve in 1865, he rode on horseback to Bethlehem. For him, the contrasting atmospheres were stunning. In America, his nation was coming apart at the seams as families turned on each other and brother fought against brother. Yet in Bethlehem, it was an entirely different scene. The peaceful silence was overwhelming as he observed the stillness of the city that evening. He would later say that the experience of that Christmas Eve night would forever sing in his soul.

Back at home three years later, he desired to write something for the children of his church about the Christmas story. The result is the hymn we know as *O Little Town of Bethlehem*. Brooks asked Lewis Redner, the church organist, to compose a melody for his poem. Though Redner struggled to find a suitable tune, the perfect melody came to his mind the evening before the Christmas service. Through the combined efforts of Brooks and Redner, the church and the world were given a new song to sing.

O little town of Bethlehem
How still we see thee lie
Above thy deep and dreamless sleep
The silent stars go by
Yet in thy dark streets shineth
The everlasting Light
The hopes and fears of all the years
Are met in thee tonight

For Christ is born of Mary
And gathered all above
While mortals sleep, the angels keep
Their watch of wondering love
O morning stars together
Proclaim the holy birth
And praises sing to God the King
And Peace to men on earth

How silently, how silently
The wondrous gift is given
So God imparts to human hearts
The blessings of His heaven
No ear may hear His coming
But in this world of sin
Where meek souls will receive him still

The dear Christ enters in

O holy Child of Bethlehem
Descend to us, we pray
Cast out our sin and enter in
Be born to us today
We hear the Christmas angels
The great glad tidings tell
O come to us, abide with us
Our Lord Emmanuel

The Pain of Christmas

Christmas can be a bittersweet season for many reasons. The excitement of Christmas is easily observed in the lights, decorations, carols, and overall joy of the season. From family gatherings to office parties and Christmas-Eve candlelight services, the thrill of worship and fellowship permeates the air with a spark of love and peace.

As joyful as Christmas is for most, however, some do not escape the bite of bitterness. For many in our world, Christmas is a time to be *endured* rather than enjoyed. It can be a heavy reality of pain and disappointment. The harshness of Christmas is experienced by every family who has lost a loved one, leaving an empty chair around the table for Christmas dinner. It is felt by every member of the military who awakens Christmas morning thousands of miles from home with nothing more than pictures and a care package for comfort. The pain is also endured by those whose house, once filled with the hustle and bustle of family, is now far too quiet. Christmas is indeed a season of joy, but not one void of pain.

All over the globe, many suffer some degree of pain at Christmas, whether they are a believer or not. But for the Christian, the pain of Christmas has a deeper spiritual meaning. To be sure, the birth of Jesus is worthy of celebrating, both in our day and in Bethlehem two thousand years ago. However, we must also consider the pain of the season. As people called to show compassion to others, we must look for ways to bless those who are hurting. Until we understand the significance of the pain of the Christmas story, we cannot minister to a wounded world. What is the pain of Christmas? The Bible explains it in a conversation between a little-known prophet with Mary and Joseph.

After the birth of Jesus, Mary and Joseph followed the customs of Jewish parents in that day. In fulfillment of Genesis 17 and Leviticus 12, Jesus was circumcised at the end of eight days. Then, forty days after His birth, to fulfill the Law, Jesus was presented in the temple in dedication to God. This ceremony required an offering given by the parents as a redemption price for the firstborn child. It is fascinating to consider that Mary and Joseph paid but five shekels to redeem the One who would one day redeem them with His own precious blood (1 Peter 1:18-19).

Scripture specifies that Mary and Joseph were to bring a pair of turtledoves or two young pigeons as a sacrifice. The typical offering required a one-year-old lamb as a burnt offering and a young bird for a sin offering. Israelite parents were to bring a sin offering, regardless of the baby's birth order. However, if a family was poor, they could offer two turtledoves or two pigeons instead. Mary and Joseph's sacrifice of two young birds reveal that they were indeed, poor. Mary and Joseph offered the sacrifice of their present financial circumstances that day. Though poor, they were not without blessing as God ordained a bittersweet encounter.

Incidentally, this also indicates that the wise men had not yet made their visit to them. If they had, Mary and Joseph would have had the resources to bring the regular offering. It should be noted that although most cherished nativity scenes include the wise men as a part of that starry night, they should be enjoyed as a symbolic part of the complete Christmas story rather than a literal representation of what took place the evening Jesus was born. These wealthy men from afar arrived at Mary and Joseph's door two years later, long after the manger was reclaimed for its customary use.

While many of the well-loved characters of Christmas represent the joy and peace of the season, there is one lesser-known man that represented both the joy and the pain. Simeon, a righteous and devout man of God, had been given a promise "by the Holy Spirit that he would not see death until he had seen the Lord's Christ" (Luke 2:25). As the Spirit led him into the temple on the day of Jesus' presentation, he, at last, beheld the One who would be the consolation of Israel.

That the Messiah would bring comfort to God's people had been well established. The Old Testament describes the hope and help that He would bring (Jeremiah 31:13, Zechariah 1:17). Despite the long delay in the fulfillment of God's promise, Simeon's belief never wavered nor waned. He no doubt wondered when it would come to pass, but he waited in faith and full expectation of one day seeing the Messiah – the One who would lead His people to a final and perfect victory.

Simeon lived in constant expectation of the coming of the Lord. And what of us? Do we do the same? The very Jesus who was promised and *has* come is the very One who promised He *will* come again. We are to live each day in anticipation of His reappearing, longing for His coming (Philippians 3:20). Just as Simeon awaited the birth of Jesus centuries ago, so we should yearn for His second advent.

As Simeon made his way to the temple that day, he knew something was different. He had no doubt been here many times before, but this day would be unlike any day he had ever experienced. This was *the* day! Led by the Holy Spirit, Simeon entered the temple where he encountered Mary, Joseph, and the baby. As he beheld baby Jesus with his own eyes, the prophet tearfully praised God. Once again, God had kept His promise.

Simeon offered a prayer at that moment, rich with words of worship and adoration. He cried out, "Lord, now you are letting your servant depart in peace, according to your word; for my eyes have seen your salvation that you have prepared in the presence of all peoples, a light for revelation to the Gentiles, and for glory to your people Israel" (Luke 2:29-32).

Having stretched out his arms to cradle the Savior of the world, Simeon is now ready to depart into the waiting arms of his heavenly Father. The word *depart* (Luke 2:29) was descriptive of a ship that set sail or a prisoner that had been freed. He is now prepared to die in peace as he rejoices in the God in whom he had placed his trust. His life's singular goal to meet the Messiah had been fulfilled. Having nothing to fear and clinging to nothing of this world, Simeon is now ready to depart and step into eternity. God has received praise from a man for whom the grave has lost its terrors, and the world has lost its charms.

Witnessing this outpouring of worship, Mary and Joseph marveled at this encounter. Simeon had told them that the Lord had promised he would meet the Messiah before he died, and once again, the favored couple observed the unmistakable evidence of God at work. With each angelic announcement and every detail sovereignly controlled, their confidence and trust in their God grew with each promise fulfilled. An impromptu time of worship commenced as Simeon held the baby and praised the Father. Mary and Joseph basked in the goodness that God was using them to raise the Messiah who had at last arrived!

Remember, however, the focus of this chapter is the *pain* of Christmas, and it has come to bear. Before he left, Simeon had a final task to fulfill. As his countenance became grave, he turned his focus to Mary. Putting aside the excitement of the present moment, his piercing words echoed through the temple. As he held Jesus in his arms, he looked to the new mother and uttered a sobering prophecy, "Behold, this child is appointed for the fall and rising of many in Israel, and for a sign that is opposed (and a sword will pierce through your own soul also)" (Luke 2:34-35).

Opposed? Pierced? Why were these burdensome words laid upon the shoulders of young Mary? As Simeon's prophecy did not include Joseph, it is likely he will not be alive by the time Jesus is betrayed, tried, and executed. In fact, when Jesus is rejected in his hometown, we read of his mother and siblings, but there is no mention of Joseph. It is clear that Mary alone will bear the agony of the crucifixion of her precious son. She will endure this pain without the comfort of her faithful husband. Mary knows for certain that they will never be a typical family and that, although there has been much celebration over the birth of her son, He is not *truly* hers, but God's.

Simeon's address to Mary is clear. While the Messiah is worthy of all praise, He will be opposed by many. Though He is the Light of the world, most will reject Him and choose to stumble in darkness. It is as John 3:19 cautions, "And this is the judgment: the light has come into the world, and people loved the darkness rather than the light because their works were evil." Jesus, Himself, will be the stumbling stone for those who do not believe (Isaiah 8:14-15) but will be the cornerstone of salvation for those who do (Isaiah 28:16).

Hearing such a bitter prophecy amidst a time of celebration, Mary must have pondered Simeon's words many times: *and a sword will pierce through your own soul also.* What could this mean? The truth is that the events of Golgotha begin in Bethlehem. Jesus will be pierced by a spear in His side, and in full view of His mother. It will be as though a sword has been thrust through her very soul.

The glory of Christmas is not fully realized apart from the pain of Christmas. There can be no true joy in Christmas without the agony of Good Friday. This innocent baby, born to bear the guilt of sinners, did so as the perfect Lamb of God, slain for our sin. His infant cry in a manger in Bethlehem is but a foreshadowing of His final cry on a cross at Calvary. Yes, it is good news that Jesus was born. It is the greatest news ever told! But the joy of Christmas is incomplete unless we celebrate the truth that Jesus came to lay down His life as a ransom.

Like Simeon, our hope is firmly rooted in the Lord. But, like Mary, we tremble at the reality of living in a hardened world. Take heart, believer! We are not without hope. Yet how does a follower of God survive in a broken and hurting world? We follow the example of Simeon and Mary. They waited patiently for the Lord's plan to unfold while living their lives in obedience to Him. So you, too, must choose to trust as you patiently wait for the Lord to accomplish His will in you.

How can this level of obedience be accomplished? We must first hope in the promises of God. The lesson of Simeon's life demonstrates that God keeps His word because He is a faithful God. The same God who promised to send His Son to us has also promised to never forsake us. The Lord has promised that we have a home in Heaven with Him. We daily hope in His promises and wait patiently for their fulfillment.

We must also trust in the power of God. While there are undoubtedly evil forces at work around us, they are not stronger than our God, who, with His spoken word, created all that exists. One day the Lord will bring all things to an appointed end. For the believer, we take heart in knowing that our God is greater than all things and that nothing can take us out of His hand.

Finally, we rest in the providence of God. For all the things we cannot know or understand, there is a God ruling over all as we find assurance in His character and goodness. The Lord has a plan, a purpose, and a timetable. We hope in His promises and trust in His power. Life has its share of pain, but it is never without purpose. One day, when we meet our Savior face-to-face as Simeon did, we will give Him praise. When every tear is forever wiped away, we will see Christ clearly. Our hearts, no longer entangled with the cares of this world, will understand the faithfulness of God in full. Yes, there will be trouble in this world. But we are of good cheer, for our Savior has overcome the world (John 16:33).

The Story of Joy to the World

If you were to take a poll of favorite Christmas carols, it would not be long before someone responds with *Joy to the World.* Even those who are not Christians and do not truly understand the meaning of Christmas will heartily sing along. It has been a Christmas standard for three hundred years.

This beloved classic was authored by Isaac Watts. One of the church's greatest hymn writers, Watts penned more than 750 songs. His enduring songs include *I Sing the Mighty Power of God, O God Our Help in Ages Past, At the Cross, When I Survey the Wondrous Cross, and We are Marching to Zion.* However, his Christmas classic was not intended as a song, and it originally had nothing to do with Christmas at all.

In 1719, Watts published a series of poems based on individual psalms from the standpoint of Christ. He desired to present Old Testament truths through the lens of New Testament knowledge, hoping to direct the focus of believers toward Jesus. The book's title was *The Psalms of David: Imitated in the Language of the New*

Testament and Applied to the Christian State and Worship. Little of his works from this volume are known today, except for one entry.

Included in the songbook of psalms was Watts' rendition of Psalm 98. The poem opens with "Joy to the world! The Lord is come." Interestingly, Isaac Watts was not even thinking of Christ's birth, but rather, of His triumphant return. He wrote his paraphrase of Psalm 98 through a Christological lens as he anticipated the day when Jesus returns to fully and perfectly rule the world with truth and grace.

The third verse speaks of the victory of Jesus on the cross as He suffered and died in the place of sinners. Just as Genesis 3 tells of the ground bearing thorns and thistles as a consequence of sin, so Jesus, Himself, wore a crown of thorns. What was given to Christ as a mocking insult was actually a picture of what He was accomplishing in His death. Jesus was bearing our sin and reversing the curse. Meditating on this truth, Watts wrote, "He comes to make His blessings flow far as the curse is found."

So while Isaac Watts would be surprised to hear his song being sung all around the world during the Christmas season, he would be glad the message of the triumph of Christ is still going forth.

We still stand in awe at the wonders of His love and repeat the sounding joy that Christ is King!

Joy to the World; the Lord is come
Let earth receive her King
Let every heart prepare Him room
And heaven and nature sing
And heaven and nature sing
And heaven and heaven and nature sing

Joy to the earth, the Savior reigns
Let men their songs employ
While fields and floods, rocks, hills, and plains
Repeat the sounding joy
Repeat the sounding joy
Repeat, repeat the sounding joy

No more let sins and sorrows grow
Nor thorns infest the ground
He comes to make His blessings flow
Far as the curse is found
Far as the curse is found
Far as, far as the curse is found

He rules the world with truth and grace
And makes the nations prove
The glories of His righteousness
And wonders of His love
And wonders of His love
And wonders, and wonders of His love

The Proclamation of Christmas

For those who have experienced the joy of parenting, it is easy to remember every moment surrounding the birth of our firstborn. I remember the people, the emotion, even the weather conditions exactly. After a long and difficult pregnancy, my wife and I were anxious to meet our baby. We had made all the appropriate preparations. He had a name, nursery, and many friends and family who were eager to get their first glimpse of him. We did not know all that his coming would entail, but we were willing to learn and expectant that our joy would only increase.

I recall wondering specific details about him. What would his face look like? Would his eyes be brown or blue? Would he remind me of my wife? Would he have some of my features? The anticipation of seeing him with our own eyes, cuddling him, and nurturing our newborn heightened with each day. We were eager to begin our parenting journey.

After checking into the hospital at the appointed time, we were holding our son more quickly than we could have imagined. We had prayed for him, talked of him, and longed to meet him. We had announced to everyone that he was coming. Then one cold wintry day, he did. With our very own eyes, we looked upon him and marveled at what God had done.

As I think back to my experience more than two decades ago, I can only imagine what it would have been like to meet the newborn Jesus. For centuries people had anticipated His arrival. They wondered when He would come, where He would live, what He would do, and if they would see Him.

And the Word became flesh and dwelt among us (John 1:14)

John chapter one answers all of these questions and more. The incredible reality of His arrival, recorded in the opening words of the Gospel of John, is clear: "And the Word became flesh and dwelt among us" (John 1:14). This may be the single most astounding statement ever made. The Messiah came in a relatable, accessible form. He walked the earth and interacted with ordinary people. He worked, ate, and slept like everyone else.

It is not that Jesus merely *appeared* to be in human form (a heresy perpetrated by a group known as the docetists); He *actually* walked the earth as God in human flesh. This simple statement that God became flesh would have shaken the first-century readers. The Greeks held that the physical realm was evil, and therefore the human body was no more than a prison in which the soul was confined. Would God really lower Himself to take on flesh? Yes! He emptied Himself so we could be full of the Spirit. He took the form of a servant so we could be heirs of the King. He was born in the likeness of men, so that we could be born again (Philippians 2:7-8).

Scripture tells us that Jesus dwelt among the people. His family, friends, and those in town were eyewitnesses to the character of the God they worshipped. Jesus took on the form of a man, partly to demonstrate how we should live. How else could the Apostle Paul have urged believers to "be imitators of me, as I am of Christ" (1 Corinthians 11:1) if not for the earthly example of Jesus? The perfect model, He dwelt among us to exemplify how we are to treat people, deal with frustration, handle opposition, and interact with sinners.

The word *dwelt* literally means to live in a tent or to make a tabernacle. We could say it this way: Jesus *tabernacled* among the people. The tabernacle in the Old Testament was of prime importance. It was the place where Israel worshipped. This sanctuary was where the presence of the Lord was made manifest. It was here that sacrifices were offered. The Israelites cherished the Old Testament location for worship. Now, Jesus is the very embodiment of all of these things. Christ is the fullness of the Godhead bodily (Colossians 2:9). He is fully God and fully man.

He is the Living Word of God, and He Himself will be the sacrifice offered to the Father as a payment for sins.

And we have seen His glory, glory as of the only Son from the Father (John 1:14)

While it's true Jesus came to provide an example for believers, His presence on earth also displays God's glory. In the days before the temple's construction, it was in the tabernacle that God's glory was made manifest. Exodus describes God's glory as a cloud that filled the tabernacle by day and a pillar of fire at night. God's glory served to instruct and guide the Israelites. They beheld God's glory in reverence, and no one dared approach. Through the birth of Jesus, this glory took on a new form…a human form, the Word made flesh.

The truth of John 1 is that now the glory of God will be on full display through Jesus Himself. With no more division between God and man, Jesus was a walking holy of holies. This reality means that the temple is no longer necessary. God's glory, no longer confined to any structure, will reach out and touch blind eyes, walk on water, and speak words of truth and comfort as the God-man, Jesus. All that the temple represented is fulfilled and embodied in Christ and made available for all to see, hear, and embrace.

Full of grace and truth (John 1:14)

As Jesus lived on the earth, He did two things we could never do: He lived in perfect truth, and He gave saving grace to sinners. These two things uniquely qualified Jesus as the only sufficient Savior. When we accept the offer of grace and believe in the truth of the gospel, we are born into the family of God. No one can achieve salvation based on personal merit because no one but Jesus qualifies. Jesus was born of a virgin and had no sin nature. His sinless life allowed Him to take our place, pay the debt we owed to God, and save us from an eternity in hell. He went to the cross to be our sin-bearer as the weight of our iniquity was placed upon His sinless shoulders and imputed His righteousness into our bankrupt account (2 Corinthians 5:21). When we had no way to pay our debt, we inherited the riches of a King.

This is the truest picture of perfect grace. As sinners, we did not deserve grace and, in fact, had earned judgment. Yet in grace, God has shown us mercy and lavishly poured out His grace to those who have faith in His Son. The poor become rich; the lost become saved; the orphan becomes part of a family. And not just any family, the forgiven are adopted into the family of the King!

Jesus unapologetically proclaimed the truth of who He was and what His purpose meant for those who would believe in Him. In John 8:24, He spoke frankly in the temple, "Unless you believe that I am he, you will die in your sins." The truth is that we are all sinners and deserving of judgment. Our culture seeks to justify sin and even celebrate it, but the reality is that we have all sinned and fallen short of God's glory (Romans 3:23). We are in debt to a holy God and have no means by which to pay it. The wages of our sin, therefore, is death (Romans 6:23). Yet, in grace, the truth of the gospel message provides a way out. God proved His love for us even while we were sinners (Romans 5:8).

Behold the Lamb of God (John 1:29)

The life Jesus lived on earth gave Him the means to demonstrate many roles that are common to man. He was a teacher, leader, friend, son, and brother. Yet His divine nature also empowered Him to be a healer and a miracle worker. He is called the door, the way, the truth, the life, the true vine, living water, and the bread of life. But His forerunner, John the Baptist, summed up His life and mission as he looked upon Christ and declared, "Behold the Lamb of God who takes away the sin of the world"(John 1:29).

The purpose of the sacrificial lamb was well known to the Jews. Over and over again, the people of God offered lambs as a payment for sin. No lamb could perfectly atone for sin as each animal was but a shadow pointing toward the substance of the true sacrifice to come. Worshippers offered up lambs as a sin offering and at

Passover. Each day at the tabernacle and eventually in the temple, lambs would be slain. The Jewish people of that day associated the imagery of a slain lamb with forgiveness. They understood the language John the Baptist used.

Jesus was the only One who could sacrifice Himself for the sins of the world. He was the only Lamb sent by God to redeem. It is true that John the Baptist had a remarkable life as well. John's parents were given notice of his coming by an angelic messenger, as were the parents of Jesus. John's birth was miraculous in that his mother Elizabeth had been barren. John, too, preached repentance. He also died for his steadfast faith. However, despite the unique circumstances surrounding his birth, John the Baptist knew he was not the promised Messiah.

John knew that his own death, though precious in the sight of God, could have no power to save. John's purpose was to prepare the way and point others to the One whose sacrificial death would buy his pardon and pay the debt of sin for all who accepted it. John knew he was called to decrease as Christ increased (John 3:30). When he refers to Jesus as the Lamb of God, he is without question foreshadowing the work necessary to satisfy God's wrath. A sacrifice to atone for sin, once and for all, was made by Jesus Christ and no other.

It is only in understanding the purpose for which Christ was born that we fully understand why Christmas is God's greatest gift. The innocent baby boy born in a manger came to die as a sacrificial lamb for the guilty. He took on human flesh so He could die in the flesh as a payment for sin. The manger bed, though joyful, was but the beginning of the mission given to Jesus to suffer and die on a cross. He exchanged the glory of Heaven for the comforting touch of a mother's arms. From the arms of His loving parents to the arms of a grateful prophet and eventually, the brutal hands of men who nailed Him to a cross, Jesus indeed was born to die. Without the cross, there is no salvation. Without the incarnation, there is no substitutionary atonement.

The Story of I Heard the Bells on Christmas Day

In 1861, the United States of America was being ripped apart by the Civil War. Its devastation permeated the nation, communities, and households. For Henry Wadsworth Longfellow, the pain of a nation's turmoil was only the beginning of what would be a devastating year for him, personally.

In July of 1861, an oppressive heat wave swept over Massachusetts, where the Longfellow's lived. Henry's wife, Fanny, decided to cut the hair of their seven-year-old daughter, Edith. To preserve the curly locks of their daughter, Fanny placed the curls in an envelope and attempted to seal it with heated wax. As she did, ignited drops of the hot wax fell on her dress. At that moment, a breeze came in through the window, and Fanny's clothing was set aflame.

Rushing frantically into her husband's study, she awakened him from a nap. He first attempted to extinguish the fire by throwing a rug on the flames. When that was unsuccessful, he threw himself on his wife. His efforts were too late to save her, and tragically,

Fanny died the very next day. The accident left Henry Longfellow severely burned on his face, hands, and arms. In fact, he would grow his famous beard in an effort to cover his scars. So significant were Mr. Longfellow's injuries, and so deep was his grief, that he could not even attend his wife's funeral.

Two years later, his eighteen-year-old son left home. Desiring to join the Union army in the Civil War, Charles Longfellow, the oldest of six children, enlisted with the 1st Massachusetts Artillery. While serving, Charles developed typhoid fever and had to return home briefly. Several months later, he rejoined the troops, but during a battle of the *Mine Run Campaign* on November 27, 1863, Charles was shot in the back. A surgeon later told his father that he missed being paralyzed by one inch.

Henry Wadsworth Longfellow would write in his journal on Christmas Day of 1861, "How inexpressibly sad are all holidays." A year later, in 1862, he would write on Christmas day, "A merry Christmas say the children, but that is no more for me." The following year at Christmas time, the year his son had been shot in battle and nearly paralyzed, Wadsworth's journal was left without entry. The sadness of the holidays was overwhelming, and the joy of the season had long since fled from him.

Things began to change in America during the Christmas season of 1864. The re-election of Abraham Lincoln, along with the prospect of the end of the Civil War, began to resurrect hope to his heart. As he heard the bells ring out on Christmas day, Longfellow, a widower of more than three years, picked up his pen and began to write. The result was a poem entitled *Christmas Bells.*

Although hope was slowly re-emerging, things were not so simple. Against the backdrop of the joyful bells of Christmas day remained the inescapable tragedy of a nation devoured by hatred and wrecked with war. One stanza of his poem reads, "And in despair, I bowed my head; 'There is no peace on earth,' I said. For hate is strong and mocks the song of peace on earth, good-will to men."

Despite the personal loss and national devastation, the hope of Christmas was coming alive within Longfellow's heart. He became convinced that the horrors of the country and even the personal loss he had suffered would not have the last word. He would conclude his poem with these hopeful words: "Then pealed the bells more loud and deep: 'God is not dead nor doth he sleep!' The wrong shall fail, the right prevail with peace on earth, good-will to men!" Four months later, the Civil War would come to a blessed end.

It would be eight years later that the poem entitled *Christmas Bells* would be set to music by John Baptiste Calkin. Two of the stanzas that dealt with the Civil War were left out, and the song eventually would be recorded with five verses. To this day, the song *I Heard the Bells on Christmas Day* is used to bring hope to the oppressed, weary, and broken-hearted. The hope of Christmas still rings out today for those who have ears to hear. The message of Christmas remains the promise of peace on earth and good-will to men.

I heard the bells on Christmas Day
Their old, familiar carols play
And wild and sweet the words repeat
Of peace on earth, good-will to men

And thought how, as the day had come
The belfries of all Christendom
Had rolled along the unbroken song
Of peace on earth, good-will to men

Till, ringing, singing on its way
The world revolved from night to day
A voice, a chime, a chant sublime
Of peace on earth, good-will to men

And in despair I bowed my head
"There is no peace on earth," I said
"For hate is strong and mocks the song
Of peace on earth, good-will to men"

Then pealed the bells more loud and deep
"God is not dead; nor doth he sleep
The wrong shall fail, the right prevail
With peace on earth, good-will to men"

Receiving the Gift

As much as I love Christmas, there is a pressure I feel every year. It's not the pressure of buying gifts and getting them wrapped. I am always prepared for those things. I make my list and check it twice. It's not even the pressure of all the parties we host. My wife and I always enjoy having people in our home, especially during the Christmas season.

While difficult to explain and maybe even harder to understand, I feel the weight of the Christmas season coming to an end. When I am listening to Christmas music in November, I feel no pressure. There is so much time left. But once you get to December, the season begins slipping away. Knowing the time is short compels me to enjoy each day, but it also creates an internal pressure that is hard to put into words. Strange, I know!

That sense of urgency raises an important question that must be asked. What are you doing with your time? Are you aware that your life, like the Christmas season, only has a limited number of days? I hope you are living with a sense of urgency, knowing that your life – like the Christmas season each year – will come and go before you know it.

Are you like the shepherds? They were invited to meet the Christ child, and they responded in obedience and worshipped. Are you like Mary? She watched the events of the birth of her Savior, thinking deeply and pondering all the events in her heart. Are you like Joseph? He trusted the plan of God even when He could not understand it all.

In all probability, most people today view Christ in the same way as people at the time of the first Christmas. So many in our culture are certainly not despising Christ but not quite worshiping Him either. Most are just stuck in the muddy grounds of indifference. Allowing the distractions of everyday life to captivate their attention, many simply miss the Christ of Christmas. Consumed by talk of careers, stock markets, and retirement plans, others fail to behold the glory of Christ. I beg you, do not miss the miracle of Christmas this year. Jesus came to earth to be our sin-bearer that through Him, we would be saved. Read that previous sentence again slowly and ponder what that means for you.

The greatest gift you can receive this Christmas season is not the coat you are hoping to get. It is not the diamond ring you have been hinting about, and it is not even the car that you dream will be delivered with a bow. The greatest gift you can receive is the grace of Jesus Christ.

The Bible teaches that if you confess your sin, have faith in Jesus Christ alone, and believe that God raised Him from the dead, you will be saved. When you receive Christ as your personal Lord and Savior, you have been given the greatest gift imaginable. If you have any questions about the truth of the gospel, take a minute and look up the following verses in the New Testament: Romans 3:23, 5:8, 6:23, and 10:9-10.

Do you feel pressure to get someone that perfect gift this year? Are you wracking your mind trying to come up with a showstopper? Have you searched high and low and failed to find that gift that no store can seem to keep in stock? None of those would be the best gift you can give this year for Christmas anyway.

I encourage you to stop and consider the true meaning of Christmas. Think about the Messianic prophecies and be encouraged that they were fulfilled in Jesus. Consider the promise God gave concerning what His Anointed One would do for you. Praise Him for keeping His Word. Meditate on the miracle of the angelic announcements and remember the response of the shepherds and the obedience of Mary and Joseph. Finally, ponder the words of Simeon and John the Baptist. The baby of Christmas was born to be the Lamb of God that would take away the sin of the world. The best gift you could give this year is simply to offer your heart to the Lord in worship and follow Him all the days of your life.

Christmas is God's greatest gift to the world. Sinners find forgiveness and salvation in the life, death, and resurrection of Jesus Christ. Will you receive the gift of grace He offers?

I pray this year you will intentionally contemplate the meaning of the season and that you will not let worldly distractions take your eyes off of Jesus. Slow down. Ponder. Obey. Worship. And may you and your family have a very Merry Christmas!